FOREWORD

The collection of "Everything Will Be Okay" travel phrasebooks published by T&P Books is designed for people traveling abroad for tourism and business. The phrasebooks contain what matters most - the essentials for basic communication. This is an indispensable set of phrases to "survive" while abroad.

This phrasebook will help you in most cases where you need to ask something, get directions, find out how much something costs, etc. It can also resolve difficult communication situations where gestures just won't help.

This book contains a lot of phrases that have been grouped according to the most relevant topics. You'll also find a mini dictionary with useful words - numbers, time, calendar, colors...

Take "Everything Will Be Okay" phrasebook with you on the road and you'll have an irreplaceable traveling companion who will help you find your way out of any situation and teach you to not fear speaking with foreigners.

TABLE OF CONTENTS

T&P Books Publishing

English-Egyptian Arabic phrasebook & mini dictionary

By Andrey Taranov

The collection of "Everything Will Be Okay" travel phrasebooks published by T&P Books is designed for people traveling abroad for tourism and business. The phrasebooks contain what matters most - the essentials for basic communication. This is an indispensable set of phrases to "survive" while abroad.

You'll also find a mini dictionary with 250 useful words required for everyday communication - the names of months and days of the week, measurements, family members, and more.

T&P Books Publishing
www.tpbooks.com

ISBN: 978-1-78716-925-8

This book is also available in E-book formats.
Please visit www.tpbooks.com or the major online bookstores.

PRONUNCIATION

T&P phonetic alphabet	Egyptian Arabic example	English example
[a]	طفّى [ṭaffa]	shorter than in ask
[ā]	إختار [eχtār]	calf, palm
[e]	ستّة [setta]	elm, medal
[i]	ميناء [minā']	shorter than in feet
[ī]	إبريل [ebrīl]	feet, meter
[o]	أغسطس [oγosṭos]	pod, John
[ō]	حلزون [ḥalazōn]	fall, bomb
[u]	كلكتا [kalkutta]	book
[ū]	جاموس [gamūs]	fuel, tuna
[b]	بداية [bedāya]	baby, book
[d]	سعادة [sa'āda]	day, doctor
[ḍ]	وضع [waḍ']	[d] pharyngeal
[ʒ]	الأرجنتين [arʒantīn]	forge, pleasure
[ẓ]	ظهر [ẓahar]	[z] pharyngeal
[f]	خفيف [χafīf]	face, food
[g]	بهجة [bahga]	game, gold
[h]	إتّجاه [ettegāh]	home, have
[ḥ]	حبّ [ḥabb]	[h] pharyngeal
[y]	ذهبي [dahaby]	yes, New York
[k]	كرسي [korsy]	clock, kiss
[l]	لمّح [lammaḥ]	lace, people
[m]	مرصد [marṣad]	magic, milk
[n]	جنوب [ganūb]	sang, thing
[p]	كابتشينو [kaputʃino]	pencil, private
[q]	وثق [wasaq]	king, club
[r]	روح [rohe]	rice, radio
[s]	سخرية [soχreya]	city, boss
[ṣ]	معصم [me'ṣam]	[s] pharyngeal
[ʃ]	عشاء ['aʃā']	machine, shark
[t]	تنوب [tanūb]	tourist, trip
[ṭ]	خريطة [χarīṭa]	[t] pharyngeal
[θ]	ماموث [mamūθ]	month, tooth
[v]	فيتنام [vietnām]	very, river
[w]	ودّع [wadda']	vase, winter
[χ]	بخيل [baχīl]	as in Scots 'loch'
[γ]	إتغدّى [etγadda]	between [g] and [h]

5

T&P phonetic alphabet	Egyptian Arabic example	English example
[z]	معزة [me'za]	zebra, please
['] (ayn)	سبعة [sab'a]	voiced pharyngeal fricative
['] (hamza)	سأل [sa'al]	glottal stop

LIST OF ABBREVIATIONS

Egyptian Arabic abbreviations

du	-	plural noun (double)
f	-	feminine noun
m	-	masculine noun
pl	-	plural

English abbreviations

ab.	-	about
adj	-	adjective
adv	-	adverb
anim.	-	animate
as adj	-	attributive noun used as adjective
e.g.	-	for example
etc.	-	et cetera
fam.	-	familiar
fem.	-	feminine
form.	-	formal
inanim.	-	inanimate
masc.	-	masculine
math	-	mathematics
mil.	-	military
n	-	noun
pl	-	plural
pron.	-	pronoun
sb	-	somebody
sing.	-	singular
sth	-	something
v aux	-	auxiliary verb
vi	-	intransitive verb
vi, vt	-	intransitive, transitive verb
vt	-	transitive verb

ARABIC
PHRASEBOOK

This section contains
important phrases that may
come in handy in various
real-life situations.
The phrasebook will help
you ask for directions, clarify
a price, buy tickets, and
order food at a restaurant

T&P Books Publishing

PHRASEBOOK
CONTENTS

T&P Books Publishing

The bare minimum

Excuse me, ...	law samaḥt, ... لو سمحت، ...
Hello.	as salāmu ʿalaykum السلام عليكم
Thank you.	ʃukran شكراً
Good bye.	maʿ as salāma مع السلامة
Yes.	naʿam نعم
No.	la لا
I don't know.	la aʿrif لا أعرف
Where? | Where to? | When?	ayna? | ila ayna? | mata? متى؟ | إلى أين؟ | أين؟

I need ...	ana ahtāʒ ila ... أنا أحتاج إلى...
I want ...	ana urīd ... أنا أريد ...
Do you have ...?	hal ʿindak ...? هل عندك...؟
Is there a ... here?	hal yūʒad huna ...? هل يوجد هنا ...؟
May I ...?	hal yumkinuni ...? هل يمكنني...؟
..., please (polite request)	... min faḍlak من فضلك ...

I'm looking for ...	abhaθ ʿan ... أبحث عن ...
restroom	ḥammām حمام
ATM	mākīnat ṣarrāf ʾāliy ماكينة صراف آلي
pharmacy (drugstore)	ṣaydaliyya صيدلية
hospital	mustaʃfa مستشفى
police station	qism aʃ ʃurṭa قسم شرطة
subway	mitru al anfāq مترو الأنفاق

taxi	taksi تاكسي
train station	maḥaṭṭat al qiṭār محطة القطار

My name is …	ismi … إسمي...
What's your name?	ma smuka? ما اسمك؟
Could you please help me?	sā'idni min faḍlak ساعدني من فضلك
I've got a problem.	'indi muʃkila عندي مشكلة
I don't feel well.	la aʃur bi χayr لا أشعر بخير
Call an ambulance!	ittaṣil bil is'āf! إتصل بالإسعاف!
May I make a call?	hal yumkinuni iʒrā' mukālama tilifūniyya? هل يمكنني إجراء مكالمة هاتفية؟

I'm sorry.	ana 'āṣif أنا آسف
You're welcome.	al 'afw العفو

I, me	aṇa أنا
you (inform.)	anta أنت
he	huwa هو
she	hiya هي
they (masc.)	hum هم
they (fem.)	hum هم
we	naḥnu نحن
you (pl)	antum أنتم
you (sg, form.)	haḍritak حضرتك

ENTRANCE	duχūl دخول
EXIT	χurūʒ خروج
OUT OF ORDER	mu'aṭṭal معطل
CLOSED	muɣlaq مغلق

OPEN	maftūḥ
	مفتوح
FOR WOMEN	lis sayyidāt
	للسيدات
FOR MEN	lir riǧāl
	للرجال

Questions

Where?	ayna? أين؟
Where to?	ila ayna? إلى أين؟
Where from?	min ayna? من أين؟
Why?	limāða? لماذا؟
For what reason?	li ayy sabab? لأي سبب؟
When?	mata? متى؟
How long?	kam waqt? كم وقتا؟
At what time?	fi ayy sā'a? في أي ساعة؟
How much?	bikam? بكم؟
Do you have ...?	hal 'indak ...? هل عندك ...؟
Where is ...?	ayna ...? أين ...؟
What time is it?	as sā'a kam? الساعة كم؟
May I make a call?	hal yumkinuni iʒrā' mukālama tilifūniyya? هل يمكنني إجراء مكالمة هاتفية؟
Who's there?	man hunāk? من هناك؟
Can I smoke here?	hal yumkinuni at tadχīn huna? هل يمكنني التدخين هنا؟
May I ...?	hal yumkinuni ...? هل يمكنني ...؟

Needs

I'd like ...	urīd an ... أريد أن...
I don't want ...	la urīd an ... لا أريد أن...
I'm thirsty.	ana 'aṭʃān أنا عطشان
I want to sleep.	urīd an anām أريد أن أنام
I want ...	urīd an ... أريد أن...
to wash up	aɣtasil أغتسل
to brush my teeth	unazzif asnāni أنظف أسناني
to rest a while	astarīḥ qalīlan أستريح قليلا
to change my clothes	uɣayyir malābisi أغير ملابسي
to go back to the hotel	arʒiʿ ilal funduq أرجع إلى الفندق
to buy ...	aʃtari ... أشتري ...
to go to ...	aðhab ila ... أذهب إلى ...
to visit ...	azūr ... أزور ...
to meet with ...	uqābil ... أقابل ...
to make a call	uʒri mukālama hātifiyya أجري مكالمة هاتفية
I'm tired.	ana ta'ibt أنا تعبت
We are tired.	naḥnu ta'ibna نحن تعبنا
I'm cold.	ana bardān أنا بردان
I'm hot.	ana ḥarrān أنا حران
I'm OK.	ana bi xayr أنا بخير

I need to make a call.	ahtāʒ ila iʒrā' mukālama hātifiyya
	أحتاج إلى إجراء مكالمة هاتفية
I need to go to the restroom.	ahtāʒ ila hammām
	أحتاج إلى حمام
I have to go.	yaʒib 'alayya an aðhab
	يجب علي أن أذهب
I have to go now.	yaʒib 'alayya an aðhab al 'ān
	يجب علي أن أذهب الآن

Asking for directions

Excuse me, ...	law samaḥt, ... لو سمحت، ...
Where is ...?	ayna ...? أين ...؟
Which way is ...?	ayna aṭ ṭarīq ila ...? أين الطريق إلى ...؟
Could you help me, please?	hal yumkinak musāʿadati, min faḍlak? هل يمكنك مساعدتي، من فضلك؟

I'm looking for ...	abḥaθ ʿan ... أبحث عن ...
I'm looking for the exit.	abḥaθ ʿan ṭarīq al ӽurūʒ أبحث عن طريق الخروج

I'm going to ...	ana ðāhib ila... أنا ذاهب إلى...
Am I going the right way to ...?	hal ana ʿalaṭ ṭarīq as saḥīḥ ila ...? هل أنا على الطريق الصحيح إلى... ؟

Is it far?	hal huwa baʿīd? هل هو بعيد؟
Can I get there on foot?	hal yumkinuni an aṣil ila hunāk māʃiyan? هل يمكنني أن أصل إلى هناك ماشيا؟

Can you show me on the map?	arīni ʿalal ӽarīta min faḍlak أريني على الخريطة من فضلك
Show me where we are right now.	arīni naḥnu ayna al ʾān أريني أين نحن الآن

Here	huna هنا
There	hunāk هناك
This way	min huna من هنا

Turn right.	inʿaṭif yamīnan إنعطف يمينا
Turn left.	inʿaṭif yasāran إنعطف يسارا
first (second, third) turn	awwal (θāni, θāliθ) ʃāriʿ أول (ثاني، ثالث) شارع

to the right	ilal yamīn
	إلى اليمين
to the left	ilal yasār
	إلى اليسار
Go straight ahead.	iðhab ilal amām mubāʃaratan
	إذهب إلى أمام مباشرة

Signs

WELCOME!	marḥaban مرحبا
ENTRANCE	duxūl دخول
EXIT	xurūʒ خروج
PUSH	idfaʻ إدفع
PULL	isḥab إسحب
OPEN	maftūḥ مفتوح
CLOSED	muɣlaq مغلق
FOR WOMEN	lis sayyidāt للسيدات
FOR MEN	lir riʒāl للرجال
GENTLEMEN, GENTS (m)	ar riʒāl الرجال
WOMEN (f)	as sayyidāt السيدات
DISCOUNTS	taxfīdāt تخفيضات
SALE	ʻūkazyūn أوكازيون
FREE	maʒʒānan مجانا
NEW!	ʒadīd! جديد!
ATTENTION!	intabih! إنتبه!
NO VACANCIES	la tūʒad ɣuraf xāliya لا توجد غرف خالية
RESERVED	maḥʒūz محجوز
ADMINISTRATION	al idāra الإدارة
STAFF ONLY	lil ʻāmilīn faqaṭ للعاملين فقط

BEWARE OF THE DOG!	iḥtaris min al kalb! إحترس من الكلب!
NO SMOKING!	mamnū' at tadχīn! ممنوع التدخين!
DO NOT TOUCH!	mamnū' al lams! ممنوع اللمس!
DANGEROUS	χaṭīr خطير
DANGER	χaṭar خطر
HIGH VOLTAGE	ʒuhd 'āli جهد عالي
NO SWIMMING!	mamnū' as sibāḥa! ممنوع السباحة!

OUT OF ORDER	mu'aṭṭal معطل
FLAMMABLE	qābil lil iʃti'āl قابل للإشتعال
FORBIDDEN	mamnū' ممنوع
NO TRESPASSING!	mamnū' at ta'addi! ممنوع التعدي!
WET PAINT	ṭilā' ḥadīθ طلاء حديث

CLOSED FOR RENOVATIONS	muɣlaq lit taʒdīdāt مغلق للتجديدات
WORKS AHEAD	amāmak a'māl fiṭ ṭarīq أمامك أعمال طرق
DETOUR	taḥwīla تحويلة

Transportation. General phrases

plane	ṭā'ira طائرة
train	qiṭār قطار
bus	ḥāfila حافلة
ferry	safīna سفينة
taxi	taksi تاكسي
car	sayyāra سيارة
schedule	ʒadwal جدول
Where can I see the schedule?	ayna yumkinuni an ara al ʒadwal? أين يمكنني أن أرى الجدول؟
workdays (weekdays)	ayyām al usbūʿ أيام الأسبوع
weekends	nihāyat al usbūʿ نهاية الأسبوع
holidays	ayyām al ʿuṭla ar rasmiyya أيام العطلة الرسمية
DEPARTURE	al muyādara المغادرة
ARRIVAL	al wusūl الوصول
DELAYED	muta'axxira متأخرة
CANCELLED	ulyiyat ألغيت
next (train, etc.)	al qādim القادم
first	al awwal الأول
last	al axīr الأخير
When is the next ...?	mata al ... al qādim? القادم؟ ... متى الـ
When is the first ...?	mata awwal ...? متى أول ...؟

When is the last ...?	mata 'āχir ...? متى آخر ...؟
transfer (change of trains, etc.)	taχyīr تغيير
to make a transfer	uχayyir أغير
Do I need to make a transfer?	hal yaʒib 'alayya taχyīr al ...? هل يجب علي تغيير الـ...؟

Buying tickets

Where can I buy tickets?	ayna yumkinuni ʃirā' tazākir? أين يمكنني شراء التذاكر؟
ticket	taðkara تذكرة
to buy a ticket	ʃirā' at taðkira شراء تذكرة
ticket price	siʕr at taðkira سعر التذكرة
Where to?	ila ayna? إلى أين؟
To what station?	ila ayy maḥaṭṭa? إلى أي محطة؟
I need ...	ana urīd ... أنا أريد ...
one ticket	taðkara wāḥida تذكرة واحدة
two tickets	taðkaratayn تذكرتين
three tickets	θalāθat taðākir ثلاث تذاكر
one-way	ðahāb faqaṭ ذهاب فقط
round-trip	ðahāban wa iyāban ذهابا وإيابا
first class	ad daraʒa al ūla الدرجة الأولى
second class	ad daraʒa aθ θāniya الدرجة الثانية
today	al yawm اليوم
tomorrow	ɣadan غدا
the day after tomorrow	baʕd ɣad بعد غد
in the morning	fis ṣabāḥ في الصباح
in the afternoon	baʕd aẓ ẓuhr بعد الظهر
in the evening	fil masā' في المساء

aisle seat	maq'ad bi ʒānib al mamarr
	مقعد بجانب الممر
window seat	maq'ad bi ʒānib an nāfiða
	مقعد بجانب النافذة
How much?	bikam?
	بكم؟
Can I pay by credit card?	hal yumkinuni an adfa' bi biṭāqat i'timān?
	هل يمكنني أن أدفع ببطاقة إئتمان؟

Bus

bus	ḥāfila حافلة
intercity bus	ḥāfila bayn al mudun حافلة بين المدن
bus stop	maḥaṭṭat al ḥāfilāt محطة الحافلات
Where's the nearest bus stop?	ayna aqrab maḥaṭṭat al ḥāfilāt? أين أقرب محطة الحافلات؟
number (bus ~, etc.)	raqm رقم
Which bus do I take to get to ...?	ayy ḥāfila ta'xuðuni ila ...? أي حافلة تأخذني إلى...؟
Does this bus go to ...?	hal taðhab haðihil ḥāfila ila ...? هل تذهب هذه الحافلة إلى...؟
How frequent are the buses?	kam marra taðhab al ḥāfilāt? كم مرة تذهب الحافلات؟
every 15 minutes	kull xams 'aʃara daqīqa كل 15 دقيقة
every half hour	kull niṣf sā'a كل نصف ساعة
every hour	kull sā'a كل ساعة
several times a day	'iddat marrāt fil yawm عدة مرات في اليوم
... times a day	... marrāt fil yawm مرأت في اليوم ...
schedule	ʒadwal جدول
Where can I see the schedule?	ayna yumkinuni an ara al ʒadwal? أين يمكنني أن أرى الجدول؟
When is the next bus?	mata al ḥāfila al qādima? متى الحافلة القادمة؟
When is the first bus?	mata awwal ḥāfila? متى أول حافلة؟
When is the last bus?	mata 'āxir ḥāfila? متى آخر حافلة؟
stop	maḥaṭṭa محطة
next stop	al maḥaṭṭa al qādima المحطة القادمة

last stop (terminus)

āxir mahatta
آخر محطة

Stop here, please.

qif huna min fadlak
قف هنا من فضلك

Excuse me, this is my stop.

law samaht, haðihi mahattati
لو سمحت، هذه محطتي

Train

train	qiṭār
	قطار
suburban train	qiṭār aḍ ḍawāḥi
	قطار الضواحي
long-distance train	qiṭār al masāfāt at ṭawīla
	قطار المسافات الطويلة
train station	maḥaṭṭat al qiṭārāt
	محطة القطارات
Excuse me, where is the exit to the platform?	law samaḥt, ayna aṭ ṭarīq ilar raṣīf
	لو سمحت، أين الطريق إلى الرصيف؟
Does this train go to ...?	ha yatawaǧǧah haðal qiṭār ila ...?
	هل يتوجه هذا القطار إلى ...؟
next train	al qiṭār al qādim
	القطار القادم
When is the next train?	mata al qiṭār al qādim?
	متى القطار القادم؟
Where can I see the schedule?	ayna yumkinuni an ara al ǧadwal?
	أين يمكنني أن أرى الجدول؟
From which platform?	min ayy raṣīf?
	من أي رصيف؟
When does the train arrive in ...?	mata yaṣil al qiṭār ila ...?
	متى يصل القطار إلى... ؟
Please help me.	sā'idni min faḍlak
	ساعدني من فضلك
I'm looking for my seat.	ana abḥaθ 'an maq'adi
	أنا أبحث عن مقعدي
We're looking for our seats.	naḥnu nabḥaθ 'an maqā'idina
	نحن نبحث عن مقاعدنا
My seat is taken.	maq'adi maʃɣūl
	مقعدي مشغول
Our seats are taken.	maqā'iduna maʃɣūla
	مقاعدنا مشغولة
I'm sorry but this is my seat.	ana 'āsif lakin haða maq'adi
	أنا آسف، ولكن هذا مقعدي
Is this seat taken?	hal haðal maq'ad maḥǧūz?
	هل هذا المقعد محجوز؟
May I sit here?	hal yumkinuni an aq'ud huna?
	هل يمكنني أن أقعد هنا؟

On the train. Dialogue (No ticket)

Ticket, please.	taðākir min faḍlak تذاكر من فضلك
I don't have a ticket.	laysat 'indi taðkira ليست عندي تذكرة
I lost my ticket.	taðkarati ḍā'at تذكرتي ضاعت
I forgot my ticket at home.	nasīt taðkirati fil bayt نسيت تذكرتي في البيت
You can buy a ticket from me.	yumkinak an taʃṭari minni taðkira يمكنك أن تشتري مني تذكرة
You will also have to pay a fine.	kama yaʒib 'alayk an tadfa' ɣarāma كما يجب عليك أن تدفع غرامة
Okay.	hasanan حسنا
Where are you going?	ila ayna taðhab? إلى أين تذهب؟
I'm going to …	aðhab ila … أذهب إلى …
How much? I don't understand.	bikam? ana la afham بكم؟ أنا لا أفهم
Write it down, please.	uktubha min faḍlak إكتبها من فضلك
Okay. Can I pay with a credit card?	hasanan. hal yumkinuni an adfa' bi bitāqat i'timān? حسنا. هل يمكنني أن أدفع ببطاقة إئتمان؟
Yes, you can.	na'am yumkinuk نعم يمكنك
Here's your receipt.	tafaḍḍal al īṣāl تفضل الإيصال
Sorry about the fine.	'āsif bi xuṣūṣ al ɣarāma أنا آسف بخصوص الغرامة
That's okay. It was my fault.	laysa hunāk ayy muʃkila. haðihi ɣalṭati ليس هناك أي مشكلة. هذه غلطتي
Enjoy your trip.	istamta' bi riḥlatak إستمتع برحلتك

Taxi

taxi	taksi تاكسي
taxi driver	sā'iq at taksi سائق التاكسي
to catch a taxi	'āxuð taksi أخذ تاكسي
taxi stand	mawqif taksi موقف تاكسي
Where can I get a taxi?	ayna yumkinuni an 'āxuð taksi? أين يمكنني أن آخذ تاكسي؟

to call a taxi	ṭalab taksi طلب تاكسي
I need a taxi.	aḥtāʒ ila taksi أحتاج إلى تاكسي
Right now.	al 'ān الآن
What is your address (location)?	ma huwa 'unwānak? ما هو عنوانك؟
My address is ...	'unwāni fi ... عنواني في ...
Your destination?	ila ayna taðhab? إلى أين تذهب؟
Excuse me, ...	law samaḥt, ... لو سمحت، ...
Are you available?	hal anta fāḍy? هل أنت فاض؟
How much is it to get to ...?	kam adfa' li aṣil ila ...? كم أدفع لأصل إلى...؟
Do you know where it is?	hal ta'rif ayna hiya? هل تعرف أين هي؟

Airport, please.	ilal maṭār min faḍlak إلى المطار من فضلك
Stop here, please.	qif huna min faḍlak قف هنا، من فضلك
It's not here.	innaha laysat huna إنها ليست هنا
This is the wrong address.	al 'unwān xāṭi' العنوان خاطئ
Turn left.	in'aṭif ilal yasār إنعطف إلى اليسار
Turn right.	in'aṭif ilal yamīn إنعطف إلى اليمين

How much do I owe you?	kam ana mudīn lak? كم أنا مدين لك؟
I'd like a receipt, please.	a'tini 'īşāl min faḍlak. أعطني إيصالا، من فضلك.
Keep the change.	iḥtafiẓ bil bāqi إحتفظ بالباقي

Would you please wait for me?	intaẓirni min faḍlak إنتظرني من فضلك
five minutes	xams daqā'iq خمس دقائق
ten minutes	'aʃar daqā'iq عشر دقائق
fifteen minutes	rub' sā'a ربع ساعة
twenty minutes	θulθ sā'a ثلث ساعة
half an hour	nişf sā'a نصف ساعة

Hotel

Hello.	as salāmu 'alaykum
	السلام عليكم
My name is ...	ismi ...
	إسمي ...
I have a reservation.	'indi ḥaʒz
	لدي حجز
I need ...	urīd ...
	أريد ...
a single room	ɣurfa li ʃaxs wāḥid
	غرفة لشخص واحد
a double room	ɣurfa li ʃaxsayn
	غرفة لشخصين
How much is that?	kam si'ruha?
	كم سعرها؟
That's a bit expensive.	hiya ɣāliya
	هي غالية
Do you have anything else?	hal 'indak xiyārāt uxra?
	هل عندك خيارات أخرى؟
I'll take it.	āxuðuha
	آخذها
I'll pay in cash.	adfa' naqdan
	أدفع نقدا
I've got a problem.	'indi muʃkila
	عندي مشكلة
My ... is broken.	... mu'aṭṭal
	... معطل
My ... is out of order.	... mu'aṭṭal /mu'aṭṭala/
	.../معطل /معطلة...
TV	at tilivizyūn
	التليفزيون
air conditioner	at takyīf
	التكييف
tap	al ḥanafiyya
	الحنفية
shower	ad duʃ
	الدوش
sink	al ḥawḍ
	الحوض
safe	al xazīna
	الخزينة

door lock	qifl al bāb
	قفل الباب
electrical outlet	maxraʒ al kahrabā'
	مخرج الكهرباء
hairdryer	muʒaffif aʃ ʃaʿr
	مجفف الشعر

I don't have …	laysa ladayya …
	ليس لدي …
water	mā'
	ماء
light	nūr
	نور
electricity	kahrabā'
	كهرباء

Can you give me …?	hal yumkinak an taʿtīni …?
	هل يمكنك أن تعطيني …؟
a towel	fūta
	فوطة
a blanket	battāniyya
	بطانية
slippers	ʃabāʃib
	شباشب
a robe	rūb
	روب
shampoo	ʃambu
	شامبو
soap	sābūn
	صابون

I'd like to change rooms.	urīd an uɣayyir al ɣurfa
	أريد أن أغير الغرفة
I can't find my key.	la astatīʿ an aʒid miftāhi
	لا أستطيع أن أجد مفتاحي
Could you open my room, please?	iftah ɣurfati min fadlak
	إفتح غرفتي من فضلك
Who's there?	man hunāk?
	من هناك؟
Come in!	tafaddal!
	!تفضل
Just a minute!	daqīqa wāhida!
	!دقيقة واحدة
Not right now, please.	laysa al 'ān min fadlak
	ليس الآن من فضلك

Come to my room, please.	taʿāla ila ɣurfati law samaht
	تعال إلى غرفتي لو سمحت
I'd like to order food service.	urīd an yuhdar at taʿām ila ɣurfati
	أريد أن يحضر الطعام إلى غرفتي
My room number is …	raqm ɣurfati huwa …
	رقم غرفتي هو …

I'm leaving …	uɣādir … أغادر ...
We're leaving …	nuɣādir … نغادر ...
right now	al 'ān الآن
this afternoon	ba'd aẓ ẓuhr بعد الظهر
tonight	masā' al yawm مساء اليوم
tomorrow	ɣadan غداً
tomorrow morning	ṣabāh al ɣad صباح الغد
tomorrow evening	masā' al ɣad مساء الغد
the day after tomorrow	ba'd ɣad بعد غد

I'd like to pay.	urīd an adfa' أريد أن أدفع
Everything was wonderful.	kull ʃay' kān rā'i' كل شيء كان رائعا
Where can I get a taxi?	ayna yumkinuni an 'āχuð taksi? أين يمكنني أن آخذ تاكسي؟
Would you call a taxi for me, please?	hal yumkinak an taṭlub li taksi law samaht? هل يمكنك أن تطلب لي تاكسي لو سمحت؟

Restaurant

Can I look at the menu, please?	hal yumkinuni an ara qā'imat aṭ ṭa'ām min faḍlak? هل يمكنني أن أرى قائمة الطعام من فضلك؟
Table for one.	mā'ida li ʃaχṣ wāḥid مائدة لشخص واحد
There are two (three, four) of us.	naḥnu iθnān (θalāθa, arba'a) نحن إثنان (ثلاثة، أربعة)

Smoking	lil mudaχχinīn للمدخنين
No smoking	li ɣayr al mudaχχinīn لغير المدخنين
Excuse me! (addressing a waiter)	law samaḥt لو سمحت
menu	qā'imat aṭ ṭa'ām قائمة الطعام
wine list	qā'imat an nabīð قائمة النبيذ
The menu, please.	al qā'ima, law samaḥt القائمة، لو سمحت

Are you ready to order?	hal anta musta'idd liṭ ṭalab? هل أنت مستعد للطلب؟
What will you have?	māða tā'χuð? ماذا تأخذ؟
I'll have ...	ana 'āχuð ... أنا آخذ ...

I'm a vegetarian.	ana nabātiy أنا نباتي
meat	laḥm لحم
fish	samak سمك
vegetables	χuḍār خضار
Do you have vegetarian dishes?	hal 'indak aṭbāq nabātiyya? هل عندك أطباق نباتية؟
I don't eat pork.	la 'ākul al χinzīr لا آكل لحم الخنزير
He /she/ doesn't eat meat.	huwa la ya'kul /hiya la ta'kul / al laḥm هو لا يأكل /هي لا تأكل/ اللحم

I am allergic to ...

'indi ḥassāsiyya ḍidda ...

عندي حساسية ضد ...

Would you please bring me ...

aḥḍir li ... min faḍlak

أحضر لي... من فضلك

salt | pepper | sugar

milḥ | filfil | sukkar

سكر ا فلفل ا ملح

coffee | tea | dessert

qahwa | ʃāy | ḥalwa

حلوى ا شاي ا قهوة

water | sparkling | plain

miyāh | ɣāziyya | bidūn ɣāz

بدون غاز ا غازية ا مياه

a spoon | fork | knife

milʕaqa | ʃawka | sikkīn

سكين ا شوكة ا ملعقة

a plate | napkin

ṭabaq | fūṭa

فوطةا طبق

Enjoy your meal!

bil hinā' waʃ ʃifā'

بالهناء والشفاء

One more, please.

wāḥida kamān law samaḥt

واحدة كمان من فضلك

It was very delicious.

kānat laðīða giddan

كانت لذيذة جدا

---

check | change | tip

ḥisāb | fakka | baqʃīʃ

بقشيشا فكةا حساب

Check, please.
(Could I have the check, please?)

aḥḍir li al ḥisāb min faḍlak?

أحضر لي الحساب من فضلك

Can I pay by credit card?

hal yumkinuni an aḍfaʕ bi biṭāqat iʾtimān?

هل يمكنني أن أدفع ببطاقة إئتمان؟

I'm sorry, there's a mistake here.

ana 'āsif, hunāk xaṭa'

أنا آسف، هناك خطأ

Shopping

Can I help you?	momken ysā'idak? هل أستطيع أن أساعدك؟
Do you have ...?	hal 'indak ...? هل عندك ...؟
I'm looking for ...	ana abḥaθ 'an ... أنا أبحث عن ...
I need ...	urīd ... أريد ...

I'm just looking.	ana faqat anẓur أنا فقط أنظر
We're just looking.	naḥnu faqat nanẓur نحن فقط ننظر
I'll come back later.	sa'a'ūd lāḥiqan سأعود لاحقا
We'll come back later.	sana'ūd lāḥiqan سنعود لاحقا
discounts | sale	taxfīdāt | 'ūkazyūn أوكازيونا تخفيضات

Would you please show me ...	arīni ... min faḍlak أريني ... من فضلك
Would you please give me ...	a'tini ... min faḍlak أعطني ... من فضلك
Can I try it on?	hal yumkin an uʒarribahu? هل يمكن أن أجربه؟
Excuse me, where's the fitting room?	law samaḥt, ayna yurfat al qiyās? لو سمحت، أين غرفة القياس؟
Which color would you like?	ayy lawn turīd? أي لون تريد؟
size | length	maqās | ṭūl طول امقاس
How does it fit?	hal yunāsibak? هل يناسبك؟

How much is it?	bikam? بكم؟
That's too expensive.	haða yāli ʒiddan هذا غال جدا
I'll take it.	aʃtarīhi أشتريه
Excuse me, where do I pay?	ayna yumkinuni an adfa' law samaḥt? أين يمكنني أن أدفع لو سمحت؟

Will you pay in cash or credit card?	hal tadfa' naqdan aw bi biṭāqat i'timān? هل تدفع نقداً أو ببطاقة إئتمان؟
In cash | with credit card	naqdan | bi biṭāqat i'timān ببطاقة إئتمان ا نقداً

Do you want the receipt?	hal turīd īṣāl? هل تريد إيصالا؟
Yes, please.	na'am, min faḍlak نعم، من فضلك
No, it's OK.	la, laysa hunāk ayy mojkila لا، ليس هناك أي مشكلة
Thank you. Have a nice day!	jukran. yawmak sa'īd شكراً. يومك سعيد

In town

Excuse me, please.	law samaḥt لو سمحت
I'm looking for ...	ana abḥaθ 'an ... أنا أبحث عن ...
the subway	mitru al anfāq مترو الأنفاق
my hotel	funduqi فندقي
the movie theater	as sinima السينما
a taxi stand	mawqif taksi موقف تاكسي
an ATM	mākīnat ṣarrāf 'āliy ماكينة صراف آلي
a foreign exchange office	maktab ṣarrāfa مكتب صرافة
an internet café	maqha intimit مقهى انترنت
... street	ʃāri'... ... شارع
this place	haðal makān هذا المكان
Do you know where ... is?	hal ta'rif ayna ...? هل تعرف أين ...؟
Which street is this?	ma ism haðaʃ ʃāri'? ما اسم هذا الشارع؟
Show me where we are right now.	arīni naḥnu ayna al 'ān? أريني أين نحن الآن؟
Can I get there on foot?	hal yumkinuni an aṣil ila hunāk māʃiyan? هل يمكنني أن أصل إلى هناك ماشيا؟
Do you have a map of the city?	hal 'indak xarīṭa lil madīna? هل عندك خريطة للمدينة؟
How much is a ticket to get in?	bikam taðkarat ad duxūl? بكم تذكرة الدخول؟
Can I take pictures here?	hal yumkinuni at taṣwīr huna? هل يمكنني التصوير هنا؟
Are you open?	hal ... maftūḥ? هل ... مفتوح؟

When do you open?

mata taftaḥūn?

متى تفتحون؟

When do you close?

mata tuɣliqūn?

متى تغلقون؟

Money

money	nuqūd نقود
cash	naqd نقد
paper money	'umla waraqiyya عملة ورقية
loose change	fakka فكة
check | change | tip	ḥisāb | fakka | baqʃīʃ بقشيش| فكة| حساب

credit card	bitāqat i'timān بطاقة إئتمان
wallet	maḥfaẓat nuqūd محفظة نقود
to buy	ʃirā' شراء
to pay	daf' دفع
fine	ɣarāma غرامة
free	maʒʒānan مجانا

Where can I buy ...?	ayna yumkinuni ʃirā' ...? أين يمكنني شراء ...؟
Is the bank open now?	hal al bank maftūḥ al 'ān? هل البنك مفتوح الآن؟
When does it open?	mata taftaḥ? متى يفتح؟
When does it close?	mata yuɣliq? متى يغلق؟

How much?	bikam? بكم؟
How much is this?	bikam haða? بكم هذا؟
That's too expensive.	haða ɣāli ʒiddan هذا غال جدا

Excuse me, where do I pay?	ayna yumkinuni an adfa' law samaḥt? أين يمكنني أن أدفع لو سمحت؟
Check, please.	al ḥisāb min faḍlak الحساب من فضلك

Can I pay by credit card?	hal yumkinuni an adfaʻ bi biṭāqat iʻtimān? هل يمكنني أن أدفع ببطاقة إئتمان؟
Is there an ATM here?	hal tūʒad huna mākīnat ṣarrāf ʼāliy? هل توجد هنا ماكينة صراف آلي؟
I'm looking for an ATM.	ana abḥaθ ʻan mākīnat ṣarrāf ʼāliy أنا أبحث عن ماكينة صراف آلي

I'm looking for a foreign exchange office.	ana abḥaθ ʻan maktab ṣarrāfa أنا أبحث عن مكتب صرافة
I'd like to change ...	urīd taɣyīr ... أريد تغيير ...
What is the exchange rate?	kam siʻr al ʻumla? كم سعر العملة؟
Do you need my passport?	hal taḥtāʒ ila ʒawāz safari? هل تحتاج إلى جواز سفري؟

Time

What time is it?	as sā'a kam? الساعة كم؟
When?	mata? متى؟
At what time?	fi ayy sā'a? في أي ساعة؟
now | later | after ...	al 'ān | fi waqt lāhiq | ba'd ... ... بعد أ في وقت لاحقا الآن

one o'clock	as sā'a al wāhida الساعة الواحدة
one fifteen	as sā'a al wāhida wa ar rub' الساعة الواحدة والربع
one thirty	as sā'a al wāhida wa an nisf الساعة الواحدة والنصف
one forty-five	as sā'a aθ θāniya illa rub' الساعة الثانية إلا ربعا

one | two | three	al wāhida | aθ θāniya | aθ θāliθa الثالثتا الثانيتا الواحدة
four | five | six	ar rābi'a | al xāmisa | as sādisa السادسة الخامسة الرابعة
seven | eight | nine	as sābi'a | aθ θāmina | at tāsi'a التاسعتا الثامنة السابعة
ten | eleven | twelve	al 'āʃira | al hādiya 'aʃara | aθ θāniya 'aʃara الثانية عشرة أ الحادية عشرة أ العاشرة

in ...	ba'd ... ... بعد
five minutes	xams daqā'iq خمس دقائق
ten minutes	'aʃar daqā'iq عشر دقائق
fifteen minutes	rub' sā'a ربع ساعة
twenty minutes	θulθ sā'a ثلث ساعة
half an hour	nisf sā'a نصف ساعة
an hour	sā'a ساعة

in the morning	fiṣ ṣabāḥ
	في الصباح
early in the morning	fiṣ ṣabāḥ al bākir
	في الصباح الباكر
this morning	ṣabāḥ al yawm
	صباح اليوم
tomorrow morning	ṣabāḥ al ɣad
	صباح الغد

in the middle of the day	fi muntaṣif an nahār
	في منتصف النهار
in the afternoon	ba'd aẓ ẓuhr
	بعد الظهر
in the evening	fil masā'
	في المساء
tonight	masā' al yawm
	مساء اليوم

at night	bil layl
	بالليل
yesterday	amṣ
	أمس
today	al yawm
	اليوم
tomorrow	ɣadan
	غدا
the day after tomorrow	ba'd ɣad
	بعد غد

What day is it today?	fi ayy yawm naḥnu?
	في أي يوم نحن؟
It's ...	naḥnu fi ...
	نحن في ...
Monday	al iθnayn
	الإثنين
Tuesday	aθ θulāθā'
	الثلاثاء
Wednesday	al 'arbi'ā'
	الأربعاء

Thursday	al xamīs
	الخميس
Friday	al ʒum'a
	الجمعة
Saturday	as sabt
	السبت
Sunday	al aḥad
	الأحد

Greetings. Introductions

Hello.

as salāmu 'alaykum
السلام عليكم

Pleased to meet you.

ana saʿīd ǧiddan bi liqā'ik
أنا سعيد جدا بلقائك

Me too.

ana asʿad
أنا أسعد

I'd like you to meet …

awudd an uʿarrifak bi …
أود أن أعرفك بـ ...

Nice to meet you.

furṣa saʿīda
فرصة سعيدة

How are you?

kayf ḥālak?
كيف حالك؟

My name is …

ismi …
أسمي ...

His name is …

ismuhu …
إسمه ...

Her name is …

ismuha …
إسمها ...

What's your name?

ma smuka?
ما اسمك؟

What's his name?

ma smuhu?
ما اسمه؟

What's her name?

ma smuha?
ما اسمها؟

What's your last name?

ma huwa ism 'ā'ilatak?
ما هو إسم عائلتك؟

You can call me …

yumkinak an tunādīni bi…
يمكنك أن تناديني بـ....

Where are you from?

min ayna anta?
من أين أنت؟

I'm from …

ana min …
أنا من ...

What do you do for a living?

māða taʿmal?
ماذا تعمل؟

Who is this?

man haða
من هذا؟

Who is he?

man huwa?
من هو؟

Who is she?

man hiya?
من هي؟

Who are they?

man hum?
من هم؟

This is ...	haða huwa /haðihi hiya/ ... هذا هو /هذه هي... /
my friend (masc.)	ṣadīqi صديقي
my friend (fem.)	ṣadīqati صديقتي
my husband	zawʒi زوجي
my wife	zawʒati زوجتي

my father	abi أبي
my mother	ummi أمي
my brother	aχi أخي
my son	ibni إبني
my daughter	ibnati إبنتي

This is our son.	haða huwa ibnuna هذا هو ابننا
This is our daughter.	haðihi hiya ibnatuna هذه هي ابنتنا
These are my children.	haʼulāʼ awlādi هؤلاء أولادي
These are our children.	haʼulāʼ awlāduna هؤلاء أولادنا

Farewells

Good bye!
as salāmu 'alaykum
السلام عليكم

Bye! (inform.)
ma' as salāma
مع السلامة

See you tomorrow.
ilal liqā' ɣadan
إلى اللقاء غدا

See you soon.
ilal liqā'
إلى اللقاء

See you at seven.
ilal liqā' as sā'a as sābi'a
إلى اللقاء الساعة السابعة

Have fun!
atamanna laka waqtan ṭayyiban!
أتمنى لكم وقتا طيبا!

Talk to you later.
ukallimuka lāḥiqan
أكلمك لاحقا

Have a nice weekend.
'uṭlat usbū' sa'īda
عطلة أسبوع سعيدة

Good night.
taṣbaḥ 'ala ɣayr
تصبح على خير

It's time for me to go.
innahu waqt ðahābi
إنه وقت ذهابي

I have to go.
yaʒib 'alayya an aðhab
يجب علي أن أذهب

I will be right back.
sa'a'ūd ḥālan
سأعود حالا

It's late.
al waqt muta'axxar
الوقت متأخر

I have to get up early.
yaʒib 'alayya an anhaḍ bākiran
يجب علي أن أنهض باكراً

I'm leaving tomorrow.
innani uɣādir ɣadan
إنني أغادر غدا

We're leaving tomorrow.
innana nuɣādir ɣadan
إننا نغادر غدا

Have a nice trip!
riḥla sa'īda!
ارحلة سعيدة!

It was nice meeting you.
furṣa sa'īda
فرصة سعيدة

It was nice talking to you.
kān laṭīf at tahadduθ ma'ak
كان لطيفا التحدث معك

Thanks for everything.
ʃukran 'ala kull ʃay'
شكرا على كل شيء

I had a very good time.

qaḍayt waqt ʒayyidan
قضيت وقتا جيدا

We had a very good time.

qaḍayna waqt ʒayyidan
قضينا وقتا جيدا

It was really great.

kull ʃayʾ kān rāʾiʿ
كل شيء كان رائعا

I'm going to miss you.

saʾaʃtāq ilayk
سأشتاق إليك

We're going to miss you.

sanaʃtāq ilayk
سنشتاق إليك

Good luck!

bit tawfīq! maʿ as salāma!
مع السلامة! بالتوفيق!

Say hi to ...

tahīyyāti li ...
تحياتي لـ...

Foreign language

I don't understand.	anạ la ạfham أنا لا أفهم
Write it down, please.	uktubha min faḍlak إكتبها من فضلك
Do you speak ...?	hal tatakallam bi ...? هل تتكلم بـ...؟

I speak a little bit of ...	atakallam bi ... qalīlan أتكلم بـ ... قليلا
English	al inʒlīziyya الإنجليزية
Turkish	at turkiyya التركية
Arabic	al ʿarabiyya العربية
French	al faransiyya الفرنسية

German	al almāniyya الألمانية
Italian	al itāliyya الإيطالية
Spanish	al isbāniyya الإسبانية
Portuguese	al burtuɣāliyya البرتغالية
Chinese	aṣ ṣīniyya الصينية
Japanese	al yabāniyya اليابانية

Can you repeat that, please.	hal yumkinuka tikrār min faḍlak? هل يمكنك تكرار من فضلك؟
I understand.	anạ afham انا أفهم
I don't understand.	anạ la ạfham أنا لا أفهم
Please speak more slowly.	takallam bi buṭ' akθar min faḍlak تكلم ببطء أكثر من فضلك

Is that correct? (Am I saying it right?)	hal haðạ ṣaḥīḥ? هل هذا صحيح؟
What is this? (What does this mean?)	māðạ yaʿni? ماذا يعني؟

Apologies

Excuse me, please.

la tu'āχiðni min faḍlak

لا تؤاخذني من فضلك

I'm sorry.

ana 'āsif

أنا آسف

I'm really sorry.

ana 'āsif ʒiddan

أنا آسف جدا

Sorry, it's my fault.

ana 'āsif innaha ɣalṭati

أنا آسف، إنها غلطتي

My mistake.

χaṭa'i

خطئي

May I ...?

hal yumkinuni ...?

هل يمكنني ...؟

Do you mind if I ...?

hal tumāni' law ...?

هل تمانع لو ...؟

It's OK.

laysa hunāk ayy muʃkila

ليس هناك أي مشكلة

It's all right.

kull ʃay' 'ala ma yurām

كل شيء على ما يرام

Don't worry about it.

la taqlaq

لا تقلق

Agreement

Yes.
na'am
نعم

Yes, sure.
aʒl
أجل

OK (Good!)
ḥasanan
حسنا

Very well.
ʒayyid ʒiddan
جيد جداً

Certainly!
bit ta'kīd!
بالتأكيد!

I agree.
ana muwāfiq
أنا موافق

That's correct.
haða ṣaḥīḥ
هذا صحيح

That's right.
haða ṣaḥīḥ
هذا صحيح

You're right.
kalāmak ṣaḥīḥ
كلامك صحيح

I don't mind.
ana la umāni'
أنا لا أمانع

Absolutely right.
anta muḥiqq tamāman
أنت محق تماما

It's possible.
innahu min al mumkin
إنه من الممكن

That's a good idea.
innaha fikra ʒayyida
إنها فكرة جيدة

I can't say no.
la astatī' an aqūl la
لا أستطيع أن أقول لا

I'd be happy to.
sa'akūn saʿīdan
سأكون سعيدا

With pleasure.
bi kull surūr
بكل سرور

Refusal. Expressing doubt

No.

la
لا

Certainly not.

tab'an la
طبعا لا

I don't agree.

lastu muwāfiq
لست موافقا

I don't think so.

la aẓunn ðalika
لا أظن ذلك

It's not true.

laysa haða ṣaḥīḥ
ليس هذا صحيحا

You are wrong.

axta'ta
أخطأت

I think you are wrong.

aẓunn annaka axta't
أظن أنك أخطأت

I'm not sure.

lastu muta'akkid
لست متأكدا

It's impossible.

haða mustaḥīl
هذا مستحيل

Nothing of the kind (sort)!

la ʃay' min haðan naw'
لا شيء من هذا النوع

The exact opposite.

al 'aks tamāman
العكس تماما

I'm against it.

ana ḍidda ðalika
أنا ضد ذلك

I don't care.

la yuhimmuni ðalika
لا يهمني ذلك

I have no idea.

laysa ladayya ayy fikra
ليس لدي أي فكرة

I doubt it.

aʃukk fe ðalik
أشك في ذلك

Sorry, I can't.

'āsif la astaṭī'
آسف، لا أستطيع

Sorry, I don't want to.

'āsif la urīd ðalika
آسف، لا أريد ذلك

Thank you, but I don't need this.

ʃukran, wa lakinnani la aḥtāʒ ila ðalika
شكرا، ولكنني لا أحتاج إلى ذلك

It's getting late.

al waqt muta'axxar
الوقت متأخر

I have to get up early.	yaʒib ʿalayya an anhaḍ bākiran
	يجب علي أن أنهض باكراً
I don't feel well.	la aʃʿur bi xayr
	لا أشعر بخير

Expressing gratitude

Thank you.	ʃukran
	شكرا
Thank you very much.	ʃukran ʒazīlan
	شكرا جزيلا
I really appreciate it.	ana uqaddir ðalika ḥaqqan
	أنا أقدر ذلك حقا
I'm really grateful to you.	ana mumtann lak ʒiddan
	أنا ممتن لك جدا
We are really grateful to you.	naḥnu mumtannīn lak ʒiddan
	نحن ممتنون لك جدا

Thank you for your time.	ʃukran ʿala waqtak
	شكرا على وقتك
Thanks for everything.	ʃukran ʿala kull ʃay'
	شكرا على كل شيء
Thank you for ...	ʃukran ʿala ...
	شكرا على ...
your help	musāʿadatak
	مساعدتك
a nice time	al waqt al laṭīf
	الوقت اللطيف

a wonderful meal	waʒba rā'iʿa
	وجبة رائعة
a pleasant evening	amsiyya mumtiʿa
	أمسية ممتعة
a wonderful day	yawm rā'iʿ
	يوم رائع
an amazing journey	riḥla mudhiʃa
	رحلة مدهشة

Don't mention it.	la ʃukr ʿala wāʒib
	لا شكر على واجب
You are welcome.	al ʿafw
	العفو
Any time.	fi ayy waqt
	في أي وقت
My pleasure.	bi kull surūr
	بكل سرور
Forget it.	insa al amr
	إنس الأمر
Don't worry about it.	la taqlaq
	لا تقلق

Congratulations. Best wishes

Congratulations!	uhanni'uka! أهنئك!
Happy birthday!	ʿīd milād saʿīd! عيد ميلاد سعيد!
Merry Christmas!	ʿīd milād saʿīd! عيد ميلاد سعيد!
Happy New Year!	sana ʒadīda saʿīda! سنة جديدة سعيدة!
Happy Easter!	ʿīd fiṣḥ saʿīd! عيد فصح سعيد!
Happy Hanukkah!	hanūka saʿīda! هانوكا سعيدة!
I'd like to propose a toast.	awudd an aqtariḥ naxb أود أن أقترح نخبا
Cheers!	fi siḥḥatak في صحتك
Let's drink to ...!	daʿawna naʃrab fi ...! دعونا نشرب في ...!
To our success!	naʒāḥna نجاحنا
To your success!	naʒāḥak نجاحك
Good luck!	bit tawfīq! بالتوفيق!
Have a nice day!	atamanna laka nahāran saʿīdan! أتمنى لك نهارا سعيدا!
Have a good holiday!	atamanna laka ʿuṭla ṭayyiba! أتمنى لك عطلة طيبة!
Have a safe journey!	atamanna laka riḥla āmina! أتمنى لك رحلة آمنة!
I hope you get better soon!	atamanna bi annaka satataḥassan qarīban أتمنى بأنك ستتحسن قريبا

Socializing

Why are you sad?	limāða anta ḥazīn? لماذا أنت حزين؟
Smile! Cheer up!	ibtasim! !إبتسم
Are you free tonight?	hal anta ḥurr haðihil layla? هل أنت حر هذه الليلة؟

May I offer you a drink?	hal tawudd an taʃrab ʃay'? هل تود أن تشرب شيئا؟
Would you like to dance?	hal tawudd an tarquṣ? هل تود أن ترقص؟
Let's go to the movies.	daʿawna naðhab ilas sinima دعونا نذهب إلى السينما

May I invite you to …?	hal yumkinuni an adʿūk ila …? هل يمكنني أن أدعوك إلى …؟
a restaurant	maṭʿam مطعم
the movies	as sinima السينما
the theater	al masraḥ المسرح
go for a walk	tamʃiya تمشية

At what time?	fi ayy sāʿa? في أي ساعة؟
tonight	haðal masā' هذا المساء
at six	as sāʿa as sādisa الساعة السادسة
at seven	as sāʿa as sābiʿa الساعة السابعة
at eight	as sāʿa aθ θāmina الساعة الثامنة
at nine	as sāʿa at tāsiʿa الساعة التاسعة

Do you like it here?	hal yuʿʒibak al makān? هل يعجبك المكان؟
Are you here with someone?	hal anta huna maʿ aḥad? هل أنت هنا مع أحد؟
I'm with my friend.	ana maʿ ṣadīq أنا مع صديق

I'm with my friends.	ana ma' asdiqā'
	أنا مع أصدقاء
No, I'm alone.	la, ana li wahdi
	لا، أنا لوحدي

Do you have a boyfriend?	hal 'indak sadīq?
	هل عندك صديق؟
I have a boyfriend.	ana 'indi sadīq
	أنا عندي صديق
Do you have a girlfriend?	hal 'indak sadīqa?
	هل عندك صديقة؟
I have a girlfriend.	ana 'indi sadīqa
	أنا عندي صديقة

Can I see you again?	hal yumkinuni ru'yatak marra uxra?
	هل يمكنني رؤيتك مرة أخرى؟
Can I call you?	hal astatī' an attasil bik?
	هل أستطيع أن أتصل بك؟
Call me. (Give me a call.)	ittasil bi
	إتصل بي
What's your number?	ma raqmak?
	ما رقمك؟
I miss you.	aʃtāq ilayk
	أشتاق إليك

You have a beautiful name.	ismak ʒamīl
	إسمك جميل
I love you.	uhibbak
	أحبك
Will you marry me?	hal tatazawwaʒīnani?
	هل تتزوجينني؟
You're kidding!	anta tamzah!
	أنت تمزح!
I'm just kidding.	ana amzah faqat
	أنا أمزح فقط

Are you serious?	hal anta gadd?
	هل أنت جاد؟
I'm serious.	ana gādd
	أنا جاد
Really?!	sahīh?
	صحيح؟
It's unbelievable!	haða ɣayr ma'qūl!
	هذا غير معقول!
I don't believe you.	la usaddiqak
	لا أصدقك
I can't.	ana la astatī'
	أنا لا أستطيع
I don't know.	la a'rif
	أنا لا أعرف
I don't understand you.	la afhamak
	أنا لا أفهمك

Please go away.	min faḍlak iðhab min huna
	من فضلك إذهب من هنا
Leave me alone!	utrukni li waḥdi!
	أتركني لوحدي!

I can't stand him.	ana la ut_iquhu
	أنا لا أطيقه
You are disgusting!	anta muɡrif
	أنت مقرف
I'll call the police!	haṭṭlob el ʃorṭa
	سأتصل بالشرطة

Sharing impressions. Emotions

I like it.	yu'ʒibuni ðalika يعجبني ذلك
Very nice.	ʒamīl ʒiddan جميل جداً
That's great!	haða rā'i' هذا رائع
It's not bad.	la ba's bihi لا بأس به

I don't like it.	la yu'ʒibuni ðalika لا يعجبني ذلك
It's not good.	laysa ʒayyid ليس جيداً
It's bad.	haða sayyi' هذا سيء
It's very bad.	haða sayyi' ʒiddan هذا سيء جداً
It's disgusting.	haða muqrif هذا مقرف

I'm happy.	ana sa'īd /sa'īda/ أنا سعيد /سعيدة/
I'm content.	ana mabsūṭ /mabsūṭa/ أنا مبسوط /مبسوطة/
I'm in love.	ana uḥibb أنا أحب
I'm calm.	ana hādi' /hādi'a/ أنا هادئ /هادئة/
I'm bored.	aʃ'ur bil malal أشعر بالملل

I'm tired.	ana ta'bān /ta'bāna/ أنا تعبان /تعبانة/
I'm sad.	ana ḥazīn /ḥazīna/ أنا حزين /حزينة/
I'm frightened.	ana χā'if /χā'ifa/ أنا خائف /خائفة/
I'm angry.	ana ɣāḍib /ɣāḍiba/ أنا غاضب /غاضبة/
I'm worried.	ana qaliq /qaliqa/ أنا قلق /قلقة/

I'm nervous.	ana mutawattir /mutawattira/ أنا متوتر /متوترة/

I'm jealous. (envious)　　　　　　　ana ɣayūr /ɣayūra/
أنا غيور /غيورة/

I'm surprised.　　　　　　　ana mutafāʒiʾ /mutafāʒiʾa/
أنا متفاجئ /متفاجئة/

I'm perplexed.　　　　　　　ana ḥāʾir /ḥāʾira/
أنا حائر /حائرة/

Problems. Accidents

I've got a problem.	'indi muʃkila عندي مشكلة
We've got a problem.	'indana muʃkila عندنا مشكلة
I'm lost.	aḍa't ṭarīqi أضعت طريقي
I missed the last bus (train).	fātatni 'āҳir ḥāfila فاتتني آخر حافلة
I don't have any money left.	laysa ladayya ayy māl ليس لدي أي مال

I've lost my ...	faqadt ... فقدت ...
Someone stole my ...	saraqu minni ... سرقوا مني ...
passport	ʒawāz as safar جواز السفر
wallet	al mahfaẓa المحفظة
papers	al awrāq الأوراق
ticket	at taðkira التذكرة

money	an nuqūd النقود
handbag	aʃ ʃanṭa الشنطة
camera	al kamira الكاميرا
laptop	al kumbyūtir al maḥmūl الكمبيوتر المحمول
tablet computer	al kumbyūtir al lawḥiy الكمبيوتر اللوحى
mobile phone	at tilifūn al maḥmūl التليفون المحمول

Help me!	sā'idni! ساعدني!
What's happened?	māða ḥadaθ? ماذا حدث؟
fire	ḥarīqa حريقة

shooting	iṭlāq an nār
	إطلاق النار
murder	qatl
	قتل
explosion	infiʒār
	إنفجار
fight	xināqa
	خناقة

Call the police!	ittaṣil biʃ ʃurṭa!
	إتصل بالشرطة!
Please hurry up!	bi sur'a min faḍlak!
	بسرعة من فضلك!
I'm looking for the police station.	abhaθ 'an qism aʃ ʃurṭa
	أبحث عن قسم الشرطة
I need to make a call.	urīd iʒrā' mukālama ḥātifiyya
	أريد إجراء مكالمة هاتفية
May I use your phone?	hal yumkinuni an astaxdim tilifūnak?
	هل يمكنني أن أستخدم تليفونك؟

I've been …	laqat ta'arraḍt li …
	لقد تعرضت لـ...
mugged	sirqa
	سرقة
robbed	sirqa
	سرقة
raped	ixtiṣāb
	إغتصاب
attacked (beaten up)	i'tidā'
	إعتداء

Are you all right?	hal anta bi xayr?
	هل أنت بخير؟
Did you see who it was?	hal ra'ayt man kān ðalik?
	هل رأيت من كان ذلك؟
Would you be able to recognize the person?	hal tastaṭī' at ta'arruf 'alayhi?
	هل ستستطيع التعرف عليه؟
Are you sure?	hal anta muta'kked?
	هل أنت متأكد؟

Please calm down.	ihda' min faḍlak
	إهدأ من فضلك
Take it easy!	hawwin 'alayk!
	هون عليك!
Don't worry!	la taqlaq!
	لا تقلق!
Everything will be fine.	kull ʃay sayakūn 'ala ma yurām
	كل شيء سيكون على ما يرام
Everything's all right.	kull ʃay' 'ala ma yurām
	كل شيء على ما يرام
Come here, please.	ta'āla huna law samaḥt
	تعال هنا لو سمحت

I have some questions for you.

'indi lak as'ila

عندي لك أسئلة

Wait a moment, please.

intazir lahza min fadlak

إنتظر لمظة من فضلك

Do you have any I.D.?

hal 'indak bitāqa ʃaxsiyya?

هل عندك بطاقة شخصية؟

Thanks. You can leave now.

ʃukran. yumkinuka al muɣādara al 'ān

شكرا. يمكنك المغادرة الآن

Hands behind your head!

da' yadayk xalfa ra'sak!

!ضع يديك خلف رأسك

You're under arrest!

anta mawqūf!

!أنت موقوف

Health problems

Please help me.	sā'idni min faḍlak
	ساعدني من فضلق
I don't feel well.	la aʃʕur bi xayr
	لا أشعر بخير
My husband doesn't feel well.	zawʒi la yaʃʕur bi xayr
	زوجي لا يشعر بخير
My son ...	ibni ...
	إبني ...
My father ...	abi ...
	أبي ...

My wife doesn't feel well.	zawʒati la taʃʕur bi xayr
	زوجتي لا تشعر بخير
My daughter ...	ibnati ...
	إبنتي ...
My mother ...	ummi ...
	أمي ...

I've got a ...	ana 'indi ...
	أنا عندي ...
headache	ṣudā'
	صداع
sore throat	iltihāb fil halq
	إلتهاب في الحلق
stomach ache	maɣaṣ
	مغص
toothache	alam asnān
	ألم أسنان

I feel dizzy.	aʃʕur bid dawār
	أشعر بالدوار
He has a fever.	'indahu humma
	عنده حمى
She has a fever.	'indaha humma
	عندها حمى
I can't breathe.	la astaṭī' at tanaffus
	لا أستطيع التنفس

I'm short of breath.	aʃʕur bi ḍīq at tanaffus
	أشعر بضيق التنفس
I am asthmatic.	u'āni min ar rabw
	أعاني من الربو
I am diabetic.	ana 'indi maraḍ aṣ sukkar
	أنا عندي مرض السكر

I can't sleep.	la astaṭī' an anām
	لا أستطيع أن أنام
food poisoning	tasammum ɣiðā'iy
	تسمم غذائي

It hurts here.	aʃ'ur bi alam huna
	أشعر بألم هنا
Help me!	sā'idni!
	!ساعدني
I am here!	ana huna!
	!أنا هنا
We are here!	naḥnu huna!
	!نحن هنا
Get me out of here!	aχraʒūni min huna
	!أخرجوني من هنا
I need a doctor.	ana aḥtāʒ ila ṭabīb
	أنا أحتاج إلى طبيب
I can't move.	la astaṭī' an ataharrak
	لا أستطيع أن أتحرك
I can't move my legs.	la astaṭī' an uharrik riʒlayya
	لا أستطيع أن أحرك رجلي

I have a wound.	'indi ʒurḥ
	عندي جرح
Is it serious?	hal al amr χaṭīr?
	هل الأمر خطير؟
My documents are in my pocket.	awrāqi fi ʒaybi
	أوراقي في جيبي
Calm down!	ihda'!
	!إهدأ
May I use your phone?	hal yumkinuni an astaχdim tilifūnak?
	هل يمكنني أن أستخدم تليفونك؟

Call an ambulance!	ittaṣil bil is'āf!
	!إتصل بالإسعاف
It's urgent!	al amr 'āʒil!
	!الأمر عاجل
It's an emergency!	innaha ḥāla ṭāri'a!
	!إنها حالة طارئة
Please hurry up!	bi sur'a min faḍlak!
	!بسرعة من فضلك
Would you please call a doctor?	ittaṣil biṭ ṭabib min faḍlak?
	إتصل بالطبيب من فضلك؟
Where is the hospital?	ayna al mustaʃfa?
	أين المستشفى؟

How are you feeling?	kayf taʃ'ur al 'ān
	كيف تشعر الآن؟
Are you all right?	hal anta bi χayr?
	هل أنت بخير؟
What's happened?	māða hadaθ?
	ماذا حدث؟

I feel better now.

aʃur bi taḥassun al 'ān

أشعر بتحسن الآن

It's OK.

la ba's

لا بأس

It's all right.

kull ʃay' 'ala ma yurām

كل شيء على ما يرام

At the pharmacy

pharmacy (drugstore)	ṣaydaliyya صيدلية
24-hour pharmacy	ṣaydaliyya arbaʻ wa ʻiʃrīn sāʻa صيدلية 24 ساعة
Where is the closest pharmacy?	ayna aqrab ṣaydaliyya? أين أقرب صيدلية؟
Is it open now?	hal hiya maftūḥa al ʼān? هل هي مفتوحة الآن؟
At what time does it open?	mata taftaḥ? متى تفتح؟
At what time does it close?	mata tuɣliq? متى تغلق؟
Is it far?	hal hiya baʻīda? هل هي بعيدة؟
Can I get there on foot?	hal yumkinuni an aṣil ila hunāk māʃiyan? هل يمكنني أن أصل إلى هناك ماشيا؟
Can you show me on the map?	arīni ʻalal xarīṭa min faḍlak أريني على الخريطة من فضلك
Please give me something for ...	min faḍlak aʻṭini ʃayʼ li ... من فضلك أعطني شيئا لـ...
a headache	aṣ ṣudāʻ الصداع
a cough	as suʻāl السعال
a cold	al bard البرد
the flu	al influenza الأنفلوانزا
a fever	al ḥumma الحمى
a stomach ache	el maɣaṣ المغص
nausea	a ɣaθayān الغثيان
diarrhea	al ishāl الإسهال
constipation	al imsāk الإمساك
pain in the back	alam fiz ẓahr ألم في الظهر

chest pain	alam fiş şadr
	ألم في الصدر
side stitch	ɣurza ӡānibiyya
	غرزة جانبية
abdominal pain	alam fil batn
	ألم في البطن

pill	ḥabba
	حبة
ointment, cream	marham, krīm
	مرهم، كريم
syrup	ʃarāb
	شراب
spray	baxxāx
	بخاخ
drops	qatarāt
	قطرات

You need to go to the hospital.	'alayk an taðhab ilaӡ mustaʃfa
	عليك أن تذهب إلى المستشفى
health insurance	ta'mīn şiḥhiy
	تأمين صحي
prescription	waşfa tibbiyya
	وصفة طبية
insect repellant	tārid lil haʃarāt
	طارد للحشرات
Band Aid	laşqa lil ӡurūḥ
	لصقة للجروح

The bare minimum

Excuse me, ...   law samaḥt, ...
لو سمحت، ...

Hello.   as salāmu 'alaykum
السلام عليكم

Thank you.   ʃukran
شكراً

Good bye.   ma' as salāma
مع السلامة

Yes.   na'am
نعم

No.   la
لا

I don't know.   la a'rif
لا أعرف

Where? | Where to? | When?   ayna? | ila ayna? | mata?
متى؟ | إلى أين؟ | أين؟

I need ...   ana ahtāʒ ila ...
أنا أحتاج إلى...

I want ...   ana urīd ...
أنا أريد ...

Do you have ...?   hal 'indak ...?
هل عندك...؟

Is there a ... here?   hal yūʒad huna ...?
هل يوجد هنا...؟

May I ...?   hal yumkinuni ...?
هل يمكنني...؟

..., please (polite request)   ... min faḍlak
من فضلك ...

I'm looking for ...   abḥaθ 'an ...
أبحث عن ...

restroom   ḥammām
حمام

ATM   mākīnat ṣarrāf 'āliy
ماكينة صراف آلي

pharmacy (drugstore)   ṣaydaliyya
صيدلية

hospital   mustaʃfa
مستشفى

police station   qism aʃ ʃurṭa
قسم شرطة

subway   mitru al anfāq
مترو الأنفاق

taxi	taksi تاكسي
train station	maḥaṭṭat al qiṭār محطة القطار

My name is ...	ismi ... إسمي...
What's your name?	ma smuka? ما اسمك؟
Could you please help me?	sā'idni min faḍlak ساعدني من فضلك
I've got a problem.	'indi muʃkila عندي مشكلة
I don't feel well.	la aʃʕur bi χayr لا أشعر بخير
Call an ambulance!	ittaṣil bil is'āf! !إتصل بالإسعاف
May I make a call?	hal yumkinuni iӡrā' mukālama tilifūniyya? هل يمكنني إجراء مكالمة هاتفية؟

I'm sorry.	ana 'āṣif أنا آسف
You're welcome.	al 'afw العفو

I, me	ana أنا
you (inform.)	anta أنت
he	huwa هو
she	hiya هي
they (masc.)	hum هم
they (fem.)	hum هم
we	naḥnu نحن
you (pl)	antum أنتم
you (sg, form.)	ḥaḍritak حضرتك

ENTRANCE	duχūl دخول
EXIT	χurūӡ خروج
OUT OF ORDER	mu'aṭṭal معطل
CLOSED	muɣlaq مغلق

OPEN	maftūḥ
	مفتوح
FOR WOMEN	lis sayyidāt
	للسيدات
FOR MEN	lir riʒāl
	للرجال

MINI DICTIONARY

This section contains 250 useful words required for everyday communication. You will find the names of months and days of the week here. The dictionary also contains topics such as colors, measurements, family, and more

T&P Books Publishing

DICTIONARY CONTENTS

T&P Books Publishing

1. Time. Calendar

time	wa't (m)	وقت
hour	sā'a (f)	ساعة
half an hour	noṣṣ sā'a (m)	نصّ ساعة
minute	de'ī'a (f)	دقيقة
second	sanya (f)	ثانية
today (adv)	el naharda	النهارده
tomorrow (adv)	bokra	بكرة
yesterday (adv)	embāreḥ	امبارح
Monday	el etneyn (m)	الإتنين
Tuesday	el talāt (m)	التلات
Wednesday	el arbe'ā' (m)	الأربعاء
Thursday	el xamīs (m)	الخميس
Friday	el gom'a (m)	الجمعة
Saturday	el sabt (m)	السبت
Sunday	el aḥad (m)	الأحد
day	yome (m)	يوم
working day	yome 'amal (m)	يوم عمل
public holiday	agāza rasmiya (f)	أجازة رسميّة
weekend	nehāyet el osbū' (f)	نهاية الأسبوع
week	osbū' (m)	أسبوع
last week (adv)	el esbū' elly fāt	الأسبوع اللي فات
next week (adv)	el esbū' elly gayī	الأسبوع اللي جاي
in the morning	fel ṣobḥ	في الصبح
in the afternoon	ba'd el dohr	بعد الظهر
in the evening	bel leyl	بالليل
tonight (this evening)	el naharda bel leyl	النهاردة بالليل
at night	bel leyl	بالليل
midnight	noṣṣ el leyl (m)	نصّ الليل
January	yanāyer (m)	يناير
February	febrāyer (m)	فبراير
March	māres (m)	مارس
April	ebrīl (m)	إبريل
May	māyo (m)	مايو
June	yonyo (m)	يونيو
July	yolyo (m)	يوليو
August	oɣosṭos (m)	أغسطس

September	sebtamber (m)	سبتمبر
October	oktober (m)	أكتوبر
November	november (m)	نوفمبر
December	desember (m)	ديسمبر

in spring	fel rabee'	في الربيع
in summer	fel ṣeyf	في الصيف
in fall	fel ҳarīf	في الخريف
in winter	fel ʃetā'	في الشتاء

month	ʃahr (m)	شهر
season (summer, etc.)	faṣl (m)	فصل
year	sana (f)	سنة

2. Numbers. Numerals

0 zero	ṣefr	صفر
1 one	wāḥed	واحد
2 two	etneyn	إتنين
3 three	talāta	ثلاثة
4 four	arba'a	أربعة

5 five	ҳamsa	خمسة
6 six	setta	ستّة
7 seven	sab'a	سبعة
8 eight	tamanya	ثمانية
9 nine	tes'a	تسعة
10 ten	'aʃara	عشرة

11 eleven	ḥedāʃar	حداشر
12 twelve	etnāʃar	إتناشر
13 thirteen	talattāʃar	تلتّاشر
14 fourteen	arba'tāʃer	أربعتاشر
15 fifteen	ҳamastāʃer	خمستاشر

16 sixteen	settāʃar	ستّاشر
17 seventeen	saba'tāʃar	سبعتاشر
18 eighteen	tamantāʃar	تمنتاشر
19 nineteen	tes'atāʃar	تسعتاشر

20 twenty	'eʃrīn	عشرين
30 thirty	talatīn	ثلاثين
40 forty	arbe'īn	أربعين
50 fifty	ҳamsīn	خمسين

60 sixty	settīn	ستّين
70 seventy	sab'īn	سبعين
80 eighty	tamanīn	ثمانين
90 ninety	tes'īn	تسعين
100 one hundred	miya	مبّة

200 two hundred	meteyn	ميتين
300 three hundred	toltomiya	تلتميّة
400 four hundred	rob'omiya	ربعميّة
500 five hundred	χomsomiya	خمسميّة
600 six hundred	sotomiya	ستميّة
700 seven hundred	sob'omiya	سبعميّة
800 eight hundred	tomnome'a	تمنمئة
900 nine hundred	tos'omiya	تسعميّة
1000 one thousand	alf	ألف
10000 ten thousand	'aʃaret 'ālāf	عشرة آلاف
one hundred thousand	mīt alf	ميت ألف
million	millyon (m)	مليون
billion	millyār (m)	مليار

3. Humans. Family

man (adult male)	rāgel (m)	راجل
young man	ʃāb (m)	شاب
woman	set (f)	ست
girl (young woman)	bent (f)	بنت
old man	'agūz (m)	عجوز
old woman	'agūza (f)	عجوزة
mother	walda (f)	والدة
father	wāled (m)	والد
son	walad (m)	ولد
daughter	bent (f)	بنت
brother	aχ (m)	أخ
sister	oχt (f)	أخت
parents	waldeyn (du)	والدين
child	ṭefl (m)	طفل
children	aṭfāl (pl)	أطفال
stepmother	merāt el abb (f)	مرات الأب
stepfather	goze el omm (m)	جوز الأم
grandmother	gedda (f)	جدّة
grandfather	gadd (m)	جدّ
grandson	ḥafīd (m)	حفيد
granddaughter	ḥafīda (f)	حفيدة
grandchildren	aḥfād (pl)	أحفاد
uncle	'amm (m), χāl (m)	عمّ، خال
aunt	'amma (f), χāla (f)	عمّة، خالة
nephew	ibn el aχ (m), ibn el uχt (m)	إبن الأخ، إبن الأخت
niece	bint el aχ (f), bint el uχt (f)	بنت الأخ، بنت الأخت
wife	goza (f)	جوزة

husband	goze (m)	جوز
married (masc.)	metgawwez	متجوز
married (fem.)	metgawweza	متجوزة
widow	armala (f)	أرملة
widower	armal (m)	أرمل

name (first name)	esm (m)	اسم
surname (last name)	esm el 'a'ela (m)	اسم العائلة

relative	'arīb (m)	قريب
friend (masc.)	ṣadīq (m)	صديق
friendship	ṣadāqa (f)	صداقة

partner	rafī' (m)	رفيق
superior (n)	el arfa' maqāman (m)	الأرفع مقاماً
colleague	zamīl (m)	زميل
neighbors	gerān (pl)	جيران

4. Human body

body	gesm (m)	جسم
heart	'alb (m)	قلب
blood	damm (m)	دم
brain	mokχ (m)	مخ

bone	'aḍm (m)	عظم
spine (backbone)	'amūd faqry (m)	عمود فقري
rib	ḍel' (m)	ضلع
lungs	re'ateyn (du)	رئتين
skin	boʃra (m)	بشرة

head	ra's (m)	رأس
face	weʃ (m)	وش
nose	manaχīr (m)	مناخير
forehead	gabha (f)	جبهة
cheek	χadd (m)	خدّ

mouth	bo' (m)	بوء
tongue	lesān (m)	لسان
tooth	senna (f)	سنّة
lips	ʃafāyef (pl)	شفايف
chin	da''n (m)	دقن

ear	wedn (f)	ودن
neck	ra'aba (f)	رقبة
eye	'eyn (f)	عين
pupil	ḥad'a (f)	حدقة
eyebrow	ḥāgeb (m)	حاجب
eyelash	remʃ (m)	رمش
hair	ʃa'r (m)	شعر

hairstyle	tasrīḥa (f)	تسريحة
mustache	ʃanab (pl)	شنب
beard	leḥya (f)	لحية
to have (a beard, etc.)	ʿando	عنده
bald (adj)	aṣlaʿ	أصلع

hand	yad (m)	يد
arm	derāʿ (f)	دراع
finger	ṣobāʿ (m)	صباع
nail	ḍefr (m)	ضفر
palm	kaff (f)	كف

shoulder	ketf (f)	كتف
leg	regl (f)	رجل
knee	rokba (f)	ركبة
heel	kaʿb (m)	كعب
back	ḍahr (m)	ضهر

5. Clothing. Personal accessories

clothes	malābes (pl)	ملابس
coat (overcoat)	balṭo (m)	بالطو
fur coat	balṭo farww (m)	بالطو فرو
jacket (e.g., leather ~)	ʒæket (m)	جاكيت
raincoat (trenchcoat, etc.)	ʒæket lel maṭar (m)	جاكيت للمطر

shirt (button shirt)	ʾamīṣ (m)	قميص
pants	banṭalone (f)	بنطلون
suit jacket	ʒæket (f)	جاكت
suit	badla (f)	بدلة

dress (frock)	fostān (m)	فستان
skirt	ʒība (f)	جيبة
T-shirt	ti ʃirt (m)	تي شيرت
bathrobe	robe el ḥammām (m)	روب حمام
pajamas	beʒāma (f)	بيجاما
workwear	lebs el ʃoɣl (m)	لبس الشغل

underwear	malābes dāχeliya (pl)	ملابس داخلية
socks	ʃarāb (m)	شراب
bra	setyāna (f)	ستيانة
pantyhose	klone (m)	كلون
stockings (thigh highs)	gawāreb (pl)	جوارب
bathing suit	mayo (m)	مايوه

hat	ṭaʾiya (f)	طاقيّة
footwear	gezam (pl)	جزم
boots (e.g., cowboy ~)	būt (m)	بوت
heel	kaʿb (m)	كعب
shoestring	ʃerīʿṭ (m)	شريط

shoe polish	warnīʃ el gazma (m)	ورنيش الجزمة
gloves	gwanty (m)	جوانتي
mittens	gwanty men ɣeyr aṣābeʿ (m)	جوانتي من غير أصابع
scarf (muffler)	skarf (m)	سكارف
glasses (eyeglasses)	naḍḍāra (f)	نظّارة
umbrella	ʃamsiya (f)	شمسيّة
tie (necktie)	karavetta (f)	كرافتة
handkerchief	mandīl (m)	منديل
comb	meʃt (m)	مشط
hairbrush	forʃet ʃaʿr (f)	فرشة شعر
buckle	bokla (f)	بكلة
belt	ḥezām (m)	حزام
purse	ʃanṭet yad (f)	شنطة يد

6. House. Apartment

apartment	ʃa''a (f)	شقّة
room	oḍa (f)	أوضة
bedroom	oḍet el nome (f)	أوضة النوم
dining room	oḍet el sofra (f)	أوضة السفرة
living room	oḍet el esteqbāl (f)	أوضة الإستقبال
study (home office)	maktab (m)	مكتب
entry room	madχal (m)	مدخل
bathroom (room with a bath or shower)	ḥammām (m)	حمّام
half bath	ḥammām (m)	حمّام
vacuum cleaner	maknasa kahraba'iya (f)	مكنسة كهربائيّة
mop	ʃarʃūba (f)	شرشوبة
dust cloth	mamsaḥa (f)	ممسحة
short broom	ma'ʃʃa (f)	مقشّة
dustpan	lammāma (f)	لمّامة
furniture	asās (m)	أثاث
table	maktab (m)	مكتب
chair	korsy (m)	كرسي
armchair	korsy (m)	كرسي
mirror	merāya (f)	مراية
carpet	seggāda (f)	سجّادة
fireplace	daffāya (f)	دفّاية
drapes	satā'er (pl)	ستائر
table lamp	abāʒūr (f)	اباجورة
chandelier	nagafa (f)	نجفة
kitchen	maṭbaχ (m)	مطبخ
gas stove (range)	botoɣāz (m)	بوتوغاز

electric stove	forn kaharabā'y (m)	فرن كهربائي
microwave oven	mikroweyv (m)	ميكروويف
refrigerator	tallāga (f)	ثلاجة
freezer	freyzer (m)	فريزر
dishwasher	ɣassālet aṭbā' (f)	غسّالة أطباق
faucet	ḥanafiya (f)	حنفيّة
meat grinder	farrāmet laḥm (f)	فرّامة لحم
juicer	'aṣṣāra (f)	عصّارة
toaster	maḥmaṣet χobz (f)	محمصة خبز
mixer	χallāṭ (m)	خلّاط
coffee machine	makinet ṣon' el 'ahwa (f)	ماكينة صنع القهوة
kettle	ɣallāya (f)	غلّاية
teapot	barrād el ʃāy (m)	برّاد الشاي
TV set	televizion (m)	تليفزيون
VCR (video recorder)	'āla tasgīl video (f)	آلة تسجيل فيديو
iron (e.g., steam ~)	makwa (f)	مكواة
telephone	telefon (m)	تليفون